THE PANGS OF SUNDAY

BOOKS BY SHARON THESEN

Artemis Hates Romance 1980
Holding the Pose 1983
Confabulations: Poems for Malcolm Lowry 1984
The Beginning of the Long Dash 1987
The Pangs of Sunday 1990

The Pangs of Sunday

poems by

Sharon Thesen

Canadian Cataloguing in Publication Data

Thesen, Sharon, 1946-
The pangs of Sunday

Poems.
ISBN 0-7710-8552-4

I. Title.

PS8589.H47P36 1990 C811'.54 C90-093092-6
PR9199.3.T53P36 1990

The publisher would like to thank the Ontario Arts Council for its assistance.

Sent in Joanna by The Typeworks, Vancouver

Printed and bound in Canada

McClelland & Stewart Inc.
The Canadian Publishers
481 University Avenue
Toronto, Ontario M5G 2E9

to my son Jesse

Monday, Tuesday, Wednesday, Thursday, Friday, and Saturday have now passed in review before the reader; the events of each day, its hopes and fears, mortifications and pleasures, have been separately stated, and the pangs of Sunday only now remain to be described, and close the week.

Jane Austen, *Northanger Abbey*

A NOTE ON THE TEXT

A number of the poems in this book first appeared in magazines and journals, among them *The Malahat Review*, *The Capilano Review*, *Canada Poetry Review*, *Brick*, *The Raddle Moon*, *Writing*, *The Canadian Forum*, *Dandelion*, *Island*, and *CVII*. Slug Press in Vancouver originally published "Radio New France Radio" as a chapbook.

I am grateful to Pamela Banting for her fine editorial guidance and for her assistance in preparing the manuscript. Thanks also to the people at Coach House Press, Oolichan Books, and Capilano College, who over the years have given me support and encouragement. Thanks to Melanie for showing me the parrot, thanks to all my friends, and thanks especially to my husband Peter Thompson. And thanks to Barbara Woodley for the photograph.

CONTENTS

IV *The Beginning of the Long Dash* (1987)

V *The Pangs of Sunday: New Poems*

I

ARTEMIS HATES ROMANCE

(1980)

Japanese Movies

The dreamy-eyed
heading somewhere
with their load of sticks
for fire –

the wholly seminal life –

unless we lead it
leads us
toward what dark wood
where cold Snow Lady waits
with blackened teeth
to cure you
of the fear of life –

O the fear of life
stinks –

dirty snow in the dogshit early spring
& a life craved someplace else
not here –

the long hard kiss of death
beauty gives
unless she loves you

her treachery then doubled
& you don't wise up to it
until you trust her

& the snow blows away her footprints –

Jack & Jill

Your heart
aching in your head
I did not care about that.
A monstrosity of boredom.
Jack went up the hill
& Jack fell down the hill
breaking his head on the stones
of the earth.
The stones of the earth
are the petrified heads of women
mouths agape
no sound. The moon
hung fat at the top of the road
dogged my elbow turning downhill,
going home.
The not caring
cowers in front of the fear
of not caring.
My mouth tight with it,
fingers
on the steering wheel
greenish under the streetlights.

Postscript to Duncan McNaughton

. . . I feel strangely Prefigured

The tulips couldn't bend more perfectly out of
that vase like a glass spinning-top
if you'd tried. Perfect
art nouveau bend of leaves over the edges &
stems distorted in the water & glass refraction
deep inside seeming to the mind to cut them off
halfway & then they begin again
in another place about an inch to the left
– And the colour, yellow creasing the edges
of that perfect blushy red. O *natura naturans*
imagination's companion, compadre
Without Blame

*

Jess has a new jacket size 6
and as he walkt out to the car I saw
where I had rolled up the edges of the sleeves
absent-mindedly before leaving
while talking or more likely reminding
as mothers do while they zip jackets
wind scarves, tuck things in
here & there. And
the talk is poofs in the air sometimes the way
in, and what if
we could remember everything we said &
everything anybody said to us. A
photographic memory of talk.
I know what I'd do, says the lady under the
pink hairdryer, I'd shoot myself.

*

Creeley on the endings of poems.
Creeley on everything
esp. the mind's fixation on itself.
STC had that too, & he sat in front of the window
trying to stop the pain behind his eyes
as the downy hills of England rolled on out of his gaze
forever.

*

We went to the art museums of London where they checked us for
bombs in brown parcels, shopping bags, bombs disguised as
mousetraps, hidden cameras obscura, underarm holsters containing
cyanide & nerve gas, obscene doomsday weapons like ruby eyes
on a ring. How could we be suspected of so much, even of
wanting to touch the paintings / lean over those velvet ropes
& stroke the strokes of Rembrandt.

Wherever, wherever
we are   Pass the wine
but don't mess my dress

Moon
ovoid shape, egg
of moon
              curving out
sweet
kisser of stars

ladylove
             how could you

be so rich being so cold &
pure with your bruised face
looking out, swollen

belly & all.

Getting On with It

The word
Shakespeare
reaches upstairs from CBC
I shiver, don't feel
so good. Poetry,
4:50 P.M. & this
curtained light.
Shakespeare
drag yr mouldy old bones
up these stairs & tell me
what you died of,
I think
I've got it
too.

Wilkinson Road

The choice between loneliness and half-being
& love and half-being
is no choice at all
but is bitterness & nowhere to be.

Po-It-Tree

It live under the stars.

It be handsome man.

It gather the bay leaf
for a crown

It dance at the wedding party
up & down.

It love licorice ice-cream cone

It hang out at the Roller Dome

It ask the book for an answer

It feel all alone.

It feel everything It be alive

It dream under the covers &
in the car

It laugh at the Polish joke

It sing along
with the singalong.

It map the heavens

It be handsome man

It gather the bay leaf
for a crown

It dance at the wedding party
up & down.

Parts of Speech

5. Usage

Do not read these words.
There are too many words written
already. It's all been
said before, everyone knows that.
There are 31 stories, or 29, or 42,
everything is the same old story.
All you have to do is
pick up your daily newspaper
& there they are,
the same old stories.
Words everywhere. A trillion
trillion words laid end to end
would stretch around the globe
a hundred times. Equators
of words, ropes
tying the world up tight,
creasing the oceans & strangling you
in your bed at night.
Dear reader, take heed &
by the way,
will you marry me?

7. *The Argument Begins with a*

Love,
whoever do you
resemble.
Not a snake,
not a thing
in the dark.
Your appearance
brings dread to the heart,
knowledge
unasked for.
In the lamplight
your eyes are green
your inevitable wound
is red. A brown moth
pins herself
against the wall,
her wings are hers
unwished for.
Wing & heart
slide toward each other
along a trajectory
called love, exchange
for a moment,
their properties. A wing-shaped
heart. A heart-shaped
wing. A beating stillness. A
motionless weight.

8. *Grinning Away in Paradise*

Sad writing
traces the windy trees
the imaginary boat's path
zig-zagging
across the pretty
waves. In the distance
Bali Ha'i & the sound
of singing. There is no
Bali Ha'i, no distance,
no singing. There are no
voices. There is
the pavement licking up the rain
& the thought of a tongue
going with it,
the thinking.

10. *Magic*

Appearances are everything.

If you ask me no questions
I'll tell you no lies.

Dyslexia
lurks around the corner,
can make you write backwards
or not at all.

The mind
runs its tongue
around itself, tries
a phrase or two.
Wonders
if it came from the dyslexic
in the blue suit or
the younger one
in the red T-shirt
who have just appeared.

Famous dyslexics
include detectives
& brilliant stars
like Betelgeuse and Rodney Kidd.

You may be a carrier &
not know it.
You may never write backwards
or not at all
& not know it
when whammo! it
suddenly appears, & it's
on instead of no

tra instead of art
ouy instead of you
em instead of me

ouy em on tra
& all that light.

11. *Echolocation*

My son asks me
which do you think
is the smartest,
whales or humans?

& I answer,
humans.

Chittering.
Chittering.

All these poor & stupid
among such noisy & hopeless
monuments to what

endless TV show
placing a rubber head
on all of us, walk-me talk-me
dollies

          & though we can't see the moon
for the crap in the sky we get TV pictures
of the moons of Saturn
previously unheard of

                                & the Eskimos get "The Gong Show"
brought to them by Anik II &
Stayfree mini-pads, the absurdity
absorbed, this is consciousness
now

       shooting across Pacific skies
over the cold & heaving waves
the whales move through, deep

under the shadow of a boat full of scientists
reaching out with divers' instruments
to capture the chittering
sublunar subaquatic
talk.

Loose Woman Poem

A landscape
full of holes.
Women.
Pierced
ears voices piercing
the ceiling, a little choir
stung by wine:
I Fall to Pieces, and
Please Release Me.
After which I put on my old wedding band
& go to the party.
Next day 222's
& the moon falls out
of my fingernail.
The house smells like oysters
& a moon is on the loose
a woman in the bathtub   another
talking on the phone, their presence
shimmers, I'm fed up
with the wages of sin
put on some Mingus
& hepcat around

How come
it's always a question
of loss, being sick of self
displaced & frantic, chopped out
of the World of Discourse
waylaid
on the Bridge of Sighs, a net
work of connections coming down
to getting laid
or not getting laid & by whom.
Except getting laid

is not the way she thinks of it,
more like
something that her moons
can waylay waylay waylay
in the dark.

II

HOLDING THE POSE

(1983)

Discourse

A quiet night, they all are.
My kid asleep
my husband out screwing around
the cat also. Even spring
is false, crocuses sprout purple
into January sunlight,
poor little things.

Outside, at a glance
headlights dance in the alleyway
mercury vapour night entranced.

Women laughing somewhere
dogs barking. Susie splitting up
with Tom at Bino's Pancake House.

And finally there's not
all that much
you can say.

The small vocabulary
of love needs its own
thin blue dictionary.

Spiritual

City streets full of silver imports:
the rainiest May yet shifts
into a rainy June & the impatience
wears, oh it wears

black stretch pants burgundy hair
crosses on a yellow light
the silver imports stop for,
wipers wagging, oh they wag away

the rain
has a grey rinse in it,
is not water but a special
substance, yes it is

soapy & benign, leaves a foam
against the curb
where the silver imports sleep

the night away, oh they sleep
that bad old night away.

Hello Goodbye

The quiet of a silver afternoon
quickens, a magnet scattering
of books under lampshades
& in the gentle, eerie music
the skyline of Toronto. Helpless,
I yearn for this one or that one
happy in their houses or unhappy
as the case may be. This wasn't
supposed to happen, yet I miss
you all. The music holds me

& won't let go. I grow small,
diminished by all the good-natured
goodbyes, the 747's taking off,
the daily effort to solve
the puzzled heart. I miss you all
& believe and don't believe
the twisted appearance of completion
as things keep ending. The music

remembers. It hath a soft
& dying fall. God knows
the sentimental beast has spoken
& I wish you were here
anyway. In the lateness
of it all enchantment is not
a dim luxury surrounded by fools.
In the lateness of it all
a numbing silence & the rhythm
of another word written,
and another.

Season of No Bungling

It wants to say something more
like, hey, how's your life been lately
or how is your broken heart.

It is a beating thing at the typewriter
with the sound of traffic going by
and you are, we are, wedded to it.

There are accordions of moonlit mountains
supplied by the caterers, or your own choice
squeezes against the white ceiling.

Oh plans and measures.
Oh *co-supremes and stars of love*
whom are you turning to now?

In this sweet and sour season
Mozart and the incredible blossoms
dance without a permit.

A whole shape of things surrenders
and a child stands there bawling
under the sound of a jet.

Praxis

Unable to imagine a future,
imagine a future better
than now, us creatures
weeping in the abattoir
only make noise & do
not transform a single fact.
So stop crying. Get up. Go out. Leap
the mossy garden wall
the steel fence or whatever
the case may be & crash
through painted arcadias,
fragments of bliss & roses
decorating your fists.

Turquoise Carnations

Equinox light oblique in the air,
the beauty eclipsed by what
it expects of us. Is this
the juxtaposition of the real?
What shall I make for dinner and
where is my kid, the car radio on
some fatuous opinion station
titillated by the problem
of prostitutes. There is no escaping
the news, the bright systematic
voices, the banal and the beautiful
views. Embarrassing turquoise carnations
await an eye for beauty
at the corner store, perhaps
they dye them to hold something up
against the news, like poetry.
Imagine a white sport coat, and a
blue carnation – all dressed up
for the dance. And how would you know
if the blood red blossoms
are the genuine article
or whether pink strains toward beauty harder.

Chorus

Your fear
& longing as big as mine

only love lays bare its
force & promise –

heart of the rose the
petals fall away from

core of a body
as big as the world

where dreams exchange
with the turning, leaning

into you, the night
petals brushing the edges of

this dark paradise,
stony world.

Friend Holding Dream

Every night I dream
about my friends, we have many adventures
along the roads, in mountain scenery.
Meantime the phone
ringing, work to do, etc. the panic
under the thin skin pulses – I know
I should stop smoking too. My manuscript
is black, I cough arbutus trees –

The sea
ripples around us. The death of Yeats
is a ghost. The ocean wind tossed
my hair into ropes, that was a few years ago
when they discovered nature
was out there & talking
seemed to help –

Nature is bears & bears
are okay, they live in the woods. Seeing one
the best thing to do is laugh
or light your mittens on fire.
I wear grey leather driving gloves
& stop at the corner store on the way home
after a long day & all day long
there was beautiful music, the air
fizzed with the damp light of nine o'clock
& cats from under the shining bushes
of St. James Church whitely appearing –

No one adores the lyrics
of popular songs like
English teachers
parking their cars,
just before going in

there is that small choke of joy
you feel in your eyes –

        & what do I love, I love
to go to bed in a dream boat
& breathe the mountain air victorious
& worried in our yodelling socks,
vertigo and heavenly voices.

Radio New France Radio

The sky over the bus station
is mustard yellow
& greasy. 4:00, a Sunday
afternoon in March.
I was happy to be carrying
my red suitcase again
walking up Rue St. Denis
on my own two feet.
One wonders about women
who have come away alone
from a bus station
& carry their own suitcase.
Unseemly, as if a cab driver
should be putting it in the trunk
while she settles herself
in the back seat, snapping open
her powder compact
to check her teeth and hair
crossing silky knees
& lighting up a Belvedere.
I didn't have far to go
only 3 blocks, a little dizzy
from the diesel air &
tired, not from walking alone
with my suitcase
but with an embarrassment
as old as history –
the desire to explain
to that grinning punk
in the black Mustang
that this is what I chose.

At the typewriter
thinking something up
while the Saturday night cabs
honk & sidle up & down
the snowy streets.

I should probably be in one
all dolled up
in a midnight blue sequined gown
but Christ, the air in this place
so crackling & dry –
too many more sparks
& this whole town
could go up in flames.

Here the days
are grey & white and the nights
are yellow & black
& there is no sunset only twilight
all the romance indoors
all the scenery human

Pigeons guttural & iridescent
in the eaves built to imitate
some remembered vision of Normandy castle
grey stone, curving out regular & low

On Sunday nights
the walls adjacent to the dance studio
shake with yelling flamenco dancers
stomping & clapping
in that quick urgent way like a bunch
of Catholic savages, my face wavers
in the mirror when they practise
their duende

Last night at 2:30 after watching
The Great Gatsby I thought
I heard a shot then screams
from that restaurant down below
oh no not the FLQ again
referendum fever running high &
always some nut with a gun

but it must have been the wind
or *The Great Gatsby*

Even the sky
looks like a 1955 social studies textbook
old & Atlantic
carrying bits of Nova Scotian
lake, the dust of Acadia

Take my winter clothes
to the Fort Net
with the big *OUI* sign on it.
Students in black overcoats
& serious eyeglasses
gaze at waterfalls in dryers
or read *Le Devoir*, Jimmy Carter
on the use of force
& Madame must charge me
quatre dollars *pour la jupe*.
These days
when spring is still a killed thing
& the wind is full of dust
the new world gets tough
on the old
& everyone looks grim
& pays through their nose
à travers des becs.

On Saturday mornings we meet to talk
women and poetry in the heated air
the charming song of the chanteuse mocks
unwilling our heavy coats and voices bare
that wish to say the things we daren't say –
draped in fur but not in Paris, no rouged lips
or horny sailors nor poets freshly off the ships
o'erwhelmed by this our beauty that will slay
them suddenly – oh no, this place is snowy
where grey days break through paler grey
and yonder waitress moves quite slowly
encumbered by necessity. O sanctuary brave
wherein we think our little hymns to Artemis
no unencumbered song, no earthly heaven this.

Long Distance: An Octave

1.

There is no
funny grammar
of love

in Prince George
no one reads
The Pleasure of the Text

2.

The enchanted
body sings

At the centre
of the garden

a sculpted angel
from many angles

seems to dance:
material, loving.

3.

The enchanted body sings.
No birds in flight
are equal to this sound,
some half-forgotten language
of belief, they fly
silently anyway & make love

in the brightening trees.
From which blossoms fall,
tokens of their momentary
stillness. I've not spoken
for a long time. Things
happen. Later, we wake up &
test the morning, belief
momentarily intact.

4.

No love poem
this, but even so
the morning sunlight
catches at the throat
like desire & my voice
in the echoing wires
sounds false & afraid.

Because it is, & yet
I report the catalpa
blossoms strewn like
an epithalamion over
the tenderness of everything
jostled in breezes.

Nowhere else is this
sound coming from,
breathing off some satellite
in the dark, catching voices
caught in the throat
by desire, the wind's presence
trembling the blue
hydrangeas

& I am carried away
by images of loss

though I speak to you
nothing of this.

5.

We talk anyway
being human &
a fine morning
promising the blooming
of dandelions, ornamental
bushes called everlasting
beauty & so forth.

Loosened by breezes
blossoms fall
out of the trees
onto the grass.

Driftingly, reproachfully.

A wedding crown
circling the dark O
where the frisbee
used to be.

6.

Dreamboats and mercy
all over the place. Roses
made of pink kleenex
blue departures
broken things

& sweet unforgettable
Prince Charming
advancing up the sidewalk

in a panoply of mirrors.
He lifts his face
to the sun & dreams,
sidestepping blossoms.

There are words
that would introduce me,
could be advanced
like flowers
held out with both hands.

I wind & unwind
the telephone cord
coiling fingers
one by one
saying yes, yes, yes
& watching the sweet Prince
be himself.

7.

Coming from outside
an image
enchantment

wild roses, a little
grassy field

across a probable
highway. Trucks

zooming by. A man
in a glass
telephone booth

has trouble
with the coins

imagining her voice
has disappeared.

8.

Old Europe endureth
parsed
by structuralists.

Damp volumes of Petrarch
Rilke, Catullus –

one for every bird
that eats
out of an old man's
hands,

one for every
speechless lover

going home.

III

CONFABULATIONS: POEMS FOR MALCOLM LOWRY

(1984)

Clarence Malcolm Lowry is buried in the village of Ripe, in East Sussex, England, "just at the edge of the consecrated ground in the churchyard." He was 46 when he died. His body was found by his wife, Margerie, on the morning of June 27, 1957. Doctors and police meditated upon a broken gin bottle, a broken bottle of orange squash, and two empty bottles of sleeping pills, each having formerly contained approximately twenty-five three-grain sodium amytal tablets. Suicide was out of the question. A heart attack was considered likely, but the coroner, declaring it a "death by misadventure," testified at the inquest that Lowry's heart was perfectly sound, as were his liver and other organs.

I still believe that bad French wine was my nemesis. I began to improve slightly when I took to rum and gave up taking vitamins.

MALCOLM LOWRY, February 1949, Dollarton

When the fire devours itself, when the power turns against itself, it seems as if the whole being is made complete at the instant of its final ruin and the intensity of the destruction is the supreme proof, the clearest proof, of its existence.

GASTON BACHELARD, *The Psychoanalysis of Fire*

Malcolm Lowry
Late of the Bowery
His prose was flowery
And often glowery
He lived, nightly, and drank, daily,
And died playing the ukelele.

from *Selected Poems of Malcolm Lowry*

*

A dove-grey morning
soon to turn blue
as lights go out
& silent movie begins
broken projector
flapping celluloid
mind's guts churning
sweating nervous erratic
guilt, it's okay
nothing wrong I could forget
it if I could remember it
legs & arms loosened out
mouth talking
fall back fast dissolve
a light snow falling in the room.

*

At the bottom of the garden
the hidden bottle. He makes
a rectitudinous beeline
for it, plain as day
his casualness an effort.
The heat spreading
everywhere, his mind
up to tricks his face
won't believe.
His stiff walk,
bones poisoned.
How he loves it all,
the amorous snake
in the amorous grass,

the disgusted neighbour
watering fruit trees
is his best friend.
The distant tequila the key
to the day, the beauty
of all things burning
through whitened glass,
his open heart
a surgical instrument.

*

Bacchus is not
the god in this case,
innocent & vulgar –
nor demon. Spirit
a magical language
binds community
sunders same.
Spirit resembling love
hence saboteur
of same. Sweet shortcut
to quote unquote hell
through a private
blinded paradise, *spiritus*
contra spiritum.

*

His ex-heart
speaking to the woman
they call the Blessed
Virgin is busy
making deals.
He's caught up in,
in love with
the exaltation
of the error

of his ways
outside the circle
outside the unmoved
& unmoving given.
He prays anyway
for love of life
at least, among
the flickering candles
beneath the serene
blue folds of her gown
his thick tongue
beating the words
behind his teeth:
I have sunk low.
Let me sink lower still.

*

White walls sweat flies
move fast as trains.

Gripping the counter's edge
to wait it out.

Watch the little maelstrom
in the draining sink,
the mindless unfaltering
laws-of-nature
vortex. His *steps*
teetered to the left,
he could not make them
incline to the right.

It was the dark.

The dark cantina
adjacent to the Bus Terminal
where lived

the widow Gregorio
and his debt
of five centavos.

*

Stooping over the half-hidden
Tequila Anejo de Jalisco
& waving to the neighbour
he mentions the weather
& also
he's on the wagon.
The funeral wagon
I'd say, glares Mr. Quincey.
In any case
more sober when drunk
than sober.
There are three
standing on the balcony
even the raggy sunflower
is erect & opprobrious.
He resents their
incessant nervous
watchfulness.
He's afraid
they think he's a liar.

*

The five attractive garter-snakes
assemble for the concert.
He's found their tastes
run to the gloomy.
His ukulele twanging out
hymn tunes
in diminished sevenths.
The pink grass swaying.
The clouds farting thunder.

The butterfly caught
in the jaws of the cat,
pulsing wings
frantic emerald curtains.

*

Should I say
Malcolm, your name
is the sound
of clam-tracks,
the knock of kelp
on rock? Or Clarence,
wooden matches hissing
at nightfall?

There you would be
on the beach in the sun
& two seconds later
your house is in flames.
Again. Manuscripts
and bottles of gin
snatched from the hellfire
always at your heels
panting & fanged.

Correspondences
too creepy to ignore.
Or maybe just bad
ventilation, rotten
luck. You were right
about a lot of things –
this world
scissored your mind,
bone-dry shreds of ecstasy
& terror igniting
your fragile nests.

*

Darkness comes
to Niagara-on-the-Lake,
another bottle
to commemorate the turn,
a yipping dance
with the Chief-of-All-the-Mohawks,
– the fireplace living room
lined with solemn watching braves
due to arrive any minute
from the bar,
Margerie in the kitchen
supposed to play "the squaw" –
Malcolm's fun
with a red face, feathers, grim
participation, one ear out
for the rest of the tribe.

*

Mea culpa.
And the culprit
is my mother,
the nanny
who tried to smother me
one day on the cliff,
the Syphilis Museum
on Paradise Road,
my diseased eyes,
Bellevue where they put me,
my immense
imagination.
The only books in the house
Inebriety by Crabbe,
Conrad Aiken's *Blue Voyage*,
maybe two or three others.
Mea culpa.

The doctor says
manic depressive, says
compulsive neurosis
the alcohol a mask.
Language the mask –
pelado – peeled –
now it takes me
up to a whole afternoon
to find the word
I need.

*

On the third boozeless day he rose,
virtue restored. Publishers
written to. A long, less
wibberley wobberley walk
along the beach rocks.
The delicate white haze
outside now, flattened zinc
coin of sea & sun a platinum
wavering disc.
Wharf creaking in the wake
of a tug, ferns
soaking up stones. The world
his oyster.
"Welcome home," my wife
smiles, greeting me.
"Ah yes, my darling, it really is
home now. I love those curtains
you made."

*

So why not a visit to our old friend
the bootlegger
on so fine an afternoon?

The dripping path grows
pitch black. Some dogs howl
at an absent moon, no drunk
tells time. A flashlight
beam from the dead
of night finds him sprawled
on the forest floor
gobbling ferns –

spitting spores
around the names
of constellations
crawling the sky.

*

He stands his back
to her, bare torso
outlined by sea & fir trees.
The callused tops of his hands
behind him kneading
& rubbing at the tabletop
he leans against,
3-packs-a-day voice
addressing the abyss
his wife writing it down.

The shakes so bad can't hold
a pen or pencil anymore
won't eat
needs help getting dressed

*

The writing body
flashing one-sided headache,
eczema on lower limbs,
heartbeat erratic,

weight loss,
blank dreams,
fatigue an invisible thief
peels away the days
at night alternating coma
& transmitter.

*

Ferris wheel revolves
backward into black night
with Lowry the lone rider
vomiting mescal sideways
across the contrary circle
of fiesta-coloured lightbulbs

*

Where I am it is dark.

I fear the worst & alas my only friend
is the Virgin for those who have nobody with
& she is not much help.

I am being spied upon by five policemen
in black sunglasses. All day long
a vulture stares at me
from around the wash basin.
While I purify my sorrow.

Marquez shot to death
in a stupid drunken argument –
or no, they took Marquez
out of his house one afternoon
and shot him, saying *you no wrider*
you an espider.
At the time he was shaving
fresh from siesta his white shirt

on the back of a chair
rungs showing through like bones
& suddenly the dog barking –

They arrest me for drawing maps on the bar
with a finger dipped in tequila –
communist, agitator, spy – plus
no passport.

Ugly voices spatter the street
with vowels of *la mordida*.

*

In Mexican prisons the third degree
is castration. They tried that
one fine night, unsuccessfully
I regret to say.

Later we ended up in the *zocalo*
guards & all, roaring with mescal
& everyone with blue faces.

They are looking for me yet.
I practise knots
on the fringe of her yellow shawl
its softness on my legs
striped with bars of shuttered light.

*

That last night in the cantina
with Yvonne & Hugh, spectral chicken
on the Day-of-the-Dead menu
the glasses of mescal appear &
disappear as if drunk by a ghost
– or did he? or was he – ever
in love with her –

his intolerable dear friends
their intolerable dear conversation
among the thunder
& from some puzzling distance –
the pimp eyeing him in the toilet stall
chewing a marzipan coffin offers him
a stone – here,
clean yourself with this –
talk of love, talk of war
& a dark symbolic horse rears up
eyeballs blazing
against the storm.

*

The Farolito is deserted
except for a one-legged rooster
& a sleeping dog. The street
empties like a drain
into the *barranco*
where they threw the Consul's body.
Where they also throw
dead dogs & those they do not name
compañero, but rather,
pelado. Thief.

*

Bix Beiderbecke at noon.
Alternating sonoryl and straight gin,
five, ten, twenty
versions of a sentence
annealed to one broken one.
Could be anywhere – the same sea
surrounds. Triumphant lucidity
of mind, the hand steady.
Everything behind him now.
The Voyage That Never Ends

swells by a page or two,
drifts north-northwest.

*

Restless. Sonoryl.
Vitamin B. The heebie-jeebies.
Sleep for three hours dreaming
animals. *Dear Albert,*
there's at least 2,000 pages more
of stuff. Forgive me.
I am murdered by the pistils
of mauve orchids in a white vase
while bolshevik choirs sing
religious. Strychnine. Allonal.
A cumulo-nimbus cloud of
empty bottles builds in the sky,
the bruises French wine
the shiny spots mescal.
A woman eats a whole man
a man whole in the lurid light.
Forgive the tone of injured innocence,
but. Chloral. Straight rum.
Nosebleed an opened tap
pouring into my hands, tossed
like roses at the cheering crowd.
Sodium pentothal – I wake up
weeping the whole grief of the world
strangling my vocabulary.

*

Loathing Margerie
I would be dead
without her. I guess
I'd better let them
put me in the hospital
for a rest. Every day

she comes to see me
wearing high heels &
reading me censored letters.
Stayed put till I couldn't
stand it, went out one night,
a few days later
I'm in a white bed
dictating memories
to the doctor. Some of them
are pretty good
even if untrue.

For a few days
I considered having the lobotomy
but Margerie and I
figured that was a bit extreme
and I'd never write again.
I'd be forever in the past tense.

*

To be rescued from hell
you have to be in hell
so they put me
in some laboratory of it
and sit outside taking notes
every time I scream
nightmare & vomit,
unlimited supply of gin,
injections of apomorphine,
a red lightbulb
burning constantly *to increase*
the horror effect, he tells us
over his clipboard.
I was locked in.
Got so thirsty
I drank my own piss, so crazy
I saw angels on fire

laughing at me.
It wasn't so bad.
Outlasted the guy before me
by five days the first time,
sixteen the next. Told them –
the stupid bastards –
I'd had the best time of my life.

*

The poets' lake country
the final cure,
sheep in pastures grazing
& Wordsworth's daffodils
exactly the host
he said they were – oh bleak
bleak days of separation
from self & catastrophic
states of mind.
He writes with a brave face
to the old fisherman in Dollarton
birthday wishes & fondest love.
They have found a lovely cottage
in the quiet village of Ripe
& listen to music on the radio
& walk and talk with the neighbours
sometimes,
go to The Lamb for a pint
or two or twenty –
it makes no difference.
Alone in the garden
after a violent night
he kisses the bright pink faces
of peonies along the fence
tasting bees & the hereafter.

*

you say you a wrider
but we read all your wridings
dey dont make sense
you no wrider
you an espider

where I am it is dark

*

A lot of rain falling
& wasted days
but a few gins
& I can still write
a decent letter.
My personality comes & goes
like the mailman, however
& I can honestly admit
(at my age, how embarrassing)
that I have no idea
who I am. Was always
good at sea, though.
Without a storm
I'm useless.
Other than those
literary parties in New York
where they loved me,
they loved me not
there's one thing
keeps coming back:
we're on our way
to the ferry terminal,
black hangover & arguing
inlet to the left breathing off
the morning stars & Margerie
suddenly quiet

puts her hands over her face
& starts to laugh. And somehow
it all seems so comical.

*

sideways conspiracy
detonates
all things for the mouth
shattered
sucking mother night
claimed
earth & stars, sea & fire
still
a mockingbird pipes
the morning in

IV

THE BEGINNING
OF THE LONG DASH

(1987)

Poem in Memory of an Earlier Poem

A moment ago
the light was perfect

the poem itself
a perfect memory – its occasion

another light, perfection

so sudden I was there
without getting there.

They have clocks now
that talk back to you.
Malcolm Lowry
always wrote standing up
his soul wanting to avoid
being fixed –

I sympathize, my whole face
raining.

The sky presses five colours
down against
the horizon, I wander

the yard with a bag of tulip bulbs
looking for earth.

Even the sea I swam in a couple
of times, peering at freighters.

Those days it seemed
I was quicker to judge & fragile
like a rock.

The Stone

Good Friday, fragile
in the mirror, passion
in the music
on the slow radio,
the young mother next door
brings a kitchen chair outside,
lifts her face to the sun.

The first warm day in ages
of rain, cold creeks of it
ran down the windshield
as I drove home, day after day,
over bridges.

It asks to be noticed
that the sun chooses to shine –
or is it that clarity at last
will sear the clouds away
banish confusion, illuminate
the manuscript of our entangled
fingers, relaxed in moonlight –

Those silent rows of monks
come out from solitary
to labour over a complicated beauty –
how did they feel
patiently gilding the garments
& long hair of those two women
who with hands folded or clenched
in grief watch the solemn volunteers
push the stone
across the door
to his body.

Tangling the Day

Tangle the day up
which is black
does not wish
you to shine
a yellow flower
on it, if it likes
butter –

That bee it composes –
daffodils, cyclamen,
a record going round, the sound
of Haydn's piano

& the car accidents
out on Broadway
so frequent now I rather like
the sound of a small collision
& don't bother
going out to see.

The Landlord's Flower Beds

Have a penchant
for purple ink, pink
peonies. They nod
on long clean stems
in the landlord's flower beds.

Their days are numbered.
Smoke & old sayings
issue from their mouths.

The tulips are likewise high
and big, the roses almost
pull you out of bed at night –

& they are white,
yellow, red, pink, all colours
of the rainbow –

the rainbow, ah, *l'arc-en-ciel!*

She makes herself arch
over the shirts that are hanging
on the line. Their empty arms
droop like sighs but old Celeste
won't blame them for not waving
at her parade.

She tosses shadows
into blue craters of tulips
& forces a slow strict march
round paradise.

The Neighbours

The music to which the young mother
waltzes with her partner the baby
is invisible to us, eating dinner
across the way, piling mussel shells up
on our side plates.

With the toothless infant
the mother waltzes.

It is earliest spring.
The baby was a Capricorn.

The landlord's flower beds
lie fallow, bare sticks
tagged with names and colours
& by the looks of it
this year will be mostly pink.

Name-tag and twist-tie
under dark patches,
clumps of branch and twig.

Tulip bulbs
practise iconoclastic rites
while various shades of pink
enjoy their titles, a ballroom
of May in the making.

The Landlord's Tiger Lilies

A lost thing was found
on a shiny day we didn't know
was lost. Airplanes
pull tin foil off the roll of the sky
& a wandering dog
gilds the landlord's tiger lilies.

For the barren reach
of modern desire
there must be better forms
than this –
something cool,
intimate as a restaurant.

If I thought you would answer me
Rilke called to the angels,
If I thought
you would answer me.

Even so, he was wrong
not to go to his daughter's wedding
& hurting people's feelings.

Chrysanthemum Perfume

So,
what now. Ten-thirty, elevenish,
cats crouching jewel-eyed
under parked cars, catalpas
a sharp lime green X-rayed
by streetlights – birds long ago
preparing for the story of night –
torch songs –

chrysanthemums
huge white heads
blooming through thin November ice
against the fence along the path
home, to Bluebeard
it was almost that bad –

through that one particular garden
we had, 1967 or so & Jamie Reid
with the collected works of Lenin
in the basement suite
& the Narcs parked outside
in a tan-coloured Buick –

The back gate on its new hinges
neatly latched behind me,
bitter scent of chrysanthemums
grabbing like dry hands at my breath
as if they knew what I wanted
to refuse, would light my way

up the porch stairs
beside wasps asleep
in hexagons & dark forms

of the police tilting
wristwatches to streetlights –

and no mother anywhere –

Marine Life, 1970

1.

August corn, tender green & gold
against the stark jumbled backdrop
of alder, Leo roaring in the sky
upstaged by the sun that beat down
day after day
on our property. I have a photo
of myself walking back
from the garden, pregnant, one foot
in front of the other.

2.

Having babies is pushed
into the tidal heave,
your body employed by an earthquake.
The glazed infant brought forth
breathless, as if worn out
from blowing up balloons.
On shore they lay gasping
wondering what next?

& years later went down there
on purpose rubbing lotions
into the skin & lying down
on the ground. Light tracings
of hair growth mimic ocean's flow
along the body, prove we were once
marine life.

3.

Chafed waist
from damp water wings, sand
in the crotch. We haul
ourselves forward, flippers
weakly bracing
body to infinite beach.
We try to be nice,
sharing our toys.
Be bothered to give
the time of day
to those who ask,
overcome
our speech impediments.
Bronze scales drop from our bodies
in a slow rush of music
leaving ovals, triangles of fur.
At the base of the spine
the glittering remnant
of a golden, ascendant tail.

4.

When I became a mother
I was no longer mother
of the cats, Minnie
and Maurice. Oh Min
I would say, you are such
a silly kitty & would
let the tomcat step
among the dinner plates
sure, down-soft, white-clawed
marmalade feet. The marriage
terrified me, dinner & breakfast
lay on the table like torn-up telegrams,
I dreamed

karate moves from the top
of the stairs, sinister *tai chi*
among the ghostly
alders, knives
flashed in the kitchen
and lighthouses also
in the feeble night.

5.

Suddenly you were upright
rounding a corner
into a room where the Boston fern
played with the cat, where I sat
in a poor velvet armchair,
loaves of bread rising like consciousness
in the oven. You were upright
though alarmingly short,
would sooner or later
fall down & cry. Your parents
fell in love again
buying your first shoes.

6.

Watched over
by the Queen of Heaven and Earth
I took his little hand & we walked
in the direction of the park,
the corner store. Things were there
he had words for. It was a slow walk
the baby listing a bit from the reach
of his hand up to mine, at times
his whole body would twist from the toes
up. Baby steps. Oh Mother,
may I?

7.

Weaning breasts fade away.
The baby cries at the door,
falls down, gets another tooth.
The mother falls asleep reading
Women in Love, body smaller & smaller
inside the nightgown. Bad dreams
in which someone you love
leaves you. You can't figure it out –
how monstrous the indifference,
how difficult
to get his attention.
Headlights climb the bedroom wall
much later. You decide whether to pretend
to be asleep.

8.

Turning the pages of *Sexual Politics*
the sound of underlining & sighs,
bread rising, laundry folded,
baby sleeping, the things on the list
called Things To Do
all done. At the park
I watch the other mothers
who stand in bathing suits
with hands on hips –
they look like mothers,
I don't. Their limbs,
I write later,
have an unloved look
unlike mine.
A hundred pounds, elbows
he pointed out one day
like a sparrow's kneecap.

No one dives for me now –
now I come up for air
or I don't.

9.

Took you swimming
in the ocean
not very deep,
ran your body
through the water
belly down, face up
laughing under the sun bonnet.
Later you fit in my lap
as we go for a swing,
the sunny air
rushing back and forth,
mild vertigo at the height, a sad
dropping sensation
through the bottom of the arc.
I'm singing an ancient song
so softly only you can hear it
& mind a million miles away
suspended, with sand on its feet,
mouth a little open exhaling
the pale & wandering stars.

10.
September 5, 1984

Night fell
seasons come & go, hydrangeas
cast their weedy blue blossoms
over soaking September lawns
& tastes in everything shift

to a cold self-possession
the colour of TV. This child
is expert. He is his father
when he makes a wish
on a small blaze of candles,
fights me on the topic of friends.
The door opens and closes
without permission, he goes
hatless on windy days, composed
of privacies, embarrassed
when I cut the cake exclaiming
over wrapped favours
as if placed there by elves
& not myself imagining
surprise. After the ball is over
& the father has gone home
the streetlights & the moon compete
to fall asleep thinking by.

for Jesse

Women like Me

Women like me
who are nevertheless married
despite effeminate behaviour, PMS,
threatening to run away
with just an address book,
a couple of recent snapshots,
some blue silk pajamas.
Rehearsing the initials
of old boyfriends on the loose
who want them back now,
two decades of house payments
behind them. They quit
smoking, or light up
guilty in fragrant cars
as they turn slow corners
or wait for children
to cross the road.

In the Japanese restaurant
she begins to confess
that sometimes they go
for more than a week without –
& a faint sexual odour
of kelp is on our hands
as we lean toward a mutual place
filled with deep-fried tentacles,
things floating in soup,
a bit of carrot here & there –

& our big empty shoes
parked like cabs full of secrets
outside the shadowy screen
of our talking, the turning
& returning sustenance.

The Occasions

Men have talked about the world
without paying attention to the world
or to their own minds, as if
they were asleep or absent-minded.
HERACLITUS

1.

Are dim. Are a missing
of the mark. Are pretty
Chinese lanterns, fireworks
I woke to thinking
someone was stealing the piano.
Are the piano itself:
Moments musicaux
fall out of the window, scatter
like mercury all over everything.

In the Public Garden someone bends
over the roses. But for the polar bears,
orangutans, sea otters,
purple-ass baboons, the giraffe,
crocodiles, peacocks, the killer whale,
the zoo is deserted. Under the water
creatures blink and eat.

These pale pink roses
are the tenderest things.
The palest alabaster pink.
Sitting with them you understand
the perfection of all things.

Moments later amnesia, *rubato*
of a phrase of light.

2.

The phone rings, hauling you up
out of a dream. You are lightheaded,
unreal, addicted to whatever
keeps you going. Books, coffee,
poetry, someone's voice.

Across town the carpenters
lay down their tools &
drive away in dusty Thunderbirds
to a meeting in the stadium.
Someone explains his situation
at the Food Bank. Someone else
closes the curtains & opens the Scotch.
The intermittent sun
exhales a yellow breath.
Clockwise, tiny black aphids
race around the convolutions
of a rose someone aims at
with a spray gun.

The convolutions of the rose
suggest an ecstasy
untroubled by too much meaning.

Or too little.

Outside the Hudson's Bay
the Hare Krishnas are hopping
and chanting: unburdened,
ecstatic, their blue invisible deities
laugh in the air.

3.

Greek Day. The Pericles Society
Souvlaki Stand runs out early.
Solemn bouzouki bands
repeat themselves in faster measures
for the young men who dance,
naked insteps flashing among the swords,
handsome conceited heads flicking
to the left and the right.
Old mothers in black click & talk
the meat smoke rises
as if from ancient battlegrounds.
Heraclitus, dog-bitten old ghost
admonishes the crowd
to wake up & share a world
as a small plane
trailing a river of plastic words
progresses round the sky.

4.

Speaking English
we go over & over
the things that happen,
but I would rather have you
in my arms than in this conversation.

Desire and ineptitude
commit themselves to memory –
it's hard not to regret
anything. For example
coldness, a pretended indifference.
The heart transformed
to a battery.

Pairs of women
lean over restaurant tables
talking. They know everything.
Their perfume recalls to them
a certain gesture in the back seat
of a taxi in Toronto that said
I agree to this.

They fiddle with their earrings,
sufficient unto themselves
in pale summer dresses
like women who wait
for a war to end.

Or the shrimp boats
to come in. So why don't you
hurry home. The windows
are open: one to the east
& one to the west. Sirens
in the cross-breeze,
novels on the bed.

Making a Break

An open space signals
where the cat
does his business
in a far corner
of the yard, facing
the mountains,
the doctor's BMW
etherized in the alley.

Thinking of this broken-up sky
where the long wind slams around
raising to a pitch & billows
our lovely wants, or is it desire
is too serious –

The blue & white cement truck
shifts gears in vain –
starting off from nowhere
with no momentum, the ballistic
kick of a green light
or go, onto the arch
of the bridge, the ache of
the long pounce over water.

Ladies' Advice

Imageless.
All I can do
is buy another
magazine,
take advice
some of it to heart.

The grey-faced neighbour
clears his
phlegmy throat
before stooping
into the car
spits
into the lilac bush.
Like clockwork
my window shades
go up & down
at daylight
nightfall.

Serious –
or was it meticulous
old Prufrock was,
picking his way
among seashells.

He uses his
handkerchief –
gentlemen do –
large ones almost
the size of diapers.
This has always
moved me – that and
shined shoes.

New Year's

Apparently sane
with my New Year's Eve
hairdo, as the cab

is coming around
eight. No exit –

but these threads
are black & gold,
shine hard
when lights
are low – so

see you on the
windswept heath
my heart, she
chatters,
will hold up
her proper end
of things, e.g.

the conversation,
her sweet little
evening bag, his imaginary
French kiss.

Woman Reading

Every night with faint thuds
the fireworks at Expo
mutter banalities of profit and loss
like a dumb king encouraged
by his minions.
The pronouncements collapse
into swirls of pale smoke
and another blossoms
red and another green
then a long concluding space of dark.
They are quite beautiful
the way kings used to be.

Well, never mind.

On Salt Spring Island
Phyllis goes swimming, the patterns
her limbs leave in the water
are Arabic for salmon.
The phone rings & rings
but I am lost in a painting:
Liseuse sur fond noir
& two blue books the Two of Diamonds
on a white table. Inside the piano
the hard velvet hammers of beauty
wear down like teeth
and say Hey Buster!
Wake up and smell the coffee.

Up in the westward mountains
they're counting the votes
at the Socred Convention. God

help us, we murmur,
awkward tourists of the metaphysical,
tuning forks held in the air
catching the notes of utter nonsense.

A, an, the

You go to the Planetarium
and do some shopping
& then you have a coffee.

You cannot bear to read any more prose
and after the second cup of coffee
you get a pain in the lower left side.

You have taken your car in for a tune-up
and may have to wait another day
before getting it back.

You have nothing to say
and your part is crooked
and your books are overdue at the library.

You take a dress to the cleaners
& then you catch the bus
and look out the window with your purse.

The oak tree
deciphers November.
It breathes & leaves,
branches fall.
The dry sound
of their scattering
descent is of crumpled
paper surrounding the heart
of someone composing
a Dear John letter.
Piling up along the boundary
where earth meets
underground, lanterns
lighting a somewhat cheerful
way, until the
however
of the second sentence.

The Shroud of Turin

December in Vancouver.
In the mail a small brochure proclaims
the Shroud of Turin, the face of Christ
passport-sized on the cover. The nose
of Christ is long, his beard white,
his eyes closed. Auras and wounds
encircle the crown of his head.

During the day the grass is the unreal green
of moss under streetlights.
The neighbour's birch tree is going bald
from the top down; from its lower branches
dangle a few small orange leaves,
scant survivors of last night's wind.

Poor men from India deliver Christmas
flyers up and down the street.
Dogs bark from behind fences
or from a spot on the sofa
with good visibility between the drapes.
The men don't look up. The bright
flyers are glossy in the sun, they speak
of charge cards and microwaves,
nightgowns and jewels.

In the second-hand clothing store
a spectacular Christmas tree sprouts angels
and candy canes among the worn brown
trousers, old toasters, toe-sculpted shoes.

These objects are from some the source
of a fine lust & are handled with care
by the cashier, who raises her arms
to begin the folding process
of a stained white bedspread, eight dollars.

The Beginning of the Long Dash

The beginning of the long dash
following ten seconds of silence
indicates exactly ten o'clock
Pacific Standard Time.

THE NATIONAL RESEARCH COUNCIL
OFFICIAL TIME SIGNAL

1.

What happens in the big topics –
topics not tropics where suffering is
the daily basis & not
about taking a moment out to relax,
the magazines' advice on how to survive
Christmas. In the Fashion Tress beauty salon
the tree is covered with white ornaments,
angels twirl from the ceiling, a quiet crèche
in the alcove beyond the row
of pink hairdryers & old women
dozing beneath them or reading about Fergie.
Cotton-batting snow
contains miniature lights, a miniature dog
with a ribbon in its ponytail scrabbles
and barks at the window. This is
a sort of paradise: languorous, expansive,
free – until the cash register
marks eviction and pain, the grey raining street
and shoppers burdened with menus and occasions,
the obligations of merriment.
But this is the truth:
the five most compelling words
are *sex*, *free*, *cure*, *money*, and *baldness*,

a chain of conditions ranging from heaven to hell
& soul in the shed like a jar of canned heat.
The moon winks, closes her jaundiced eye,
her lockjaw & salacious grin.

3.

What being awaits us
in the land of toy soldiers
whose flesh alone is uniform
minus the smart reds, blues,
blacks and brasses of their buttons,
their chin-strap headgear and
precise swords. High on Mont Blanc
with the wind in her hair
she dreams of her lover far away,
a soldier, & inhales the scent
of alpine flowers, a goat
bleating in the distance.
A mountain goat.
This is beautiful & the topic
of myriad songs, all of which end
on a hopeful note.
Re-seeing is what we long for in absence,
from a height so great
the world is simply pattern below us,
pleasing enough. *Au revoir*
echoing among the mountain tops
in the chill wind that gathers
and floats the balloons of our thoughts.
Some are helium, some merely CO2. *Bios*
the only fit topic of speech,
not speech itself but the field of it.
In the remains of the forest
the weeping of children & animals
we don't want to hear. Not show business,
not career. Such preoccupation
verges on the obsessive, *viz.* Kurtz
from his deathbed gesturing evilly
to the forest Oh I will wring
your heart yet! Our language careers
us around the bend and so
the little tinpot boat goes too

& its crew of ragtag mercenaries.
Never mind the monkeys, their chittering
objections. The women are disturbed
at intimate tasks such as painting their bodies
in pleasing patterns. The jungle burns. We watch
it on TV neither right nor wrong
to be doing so. When the sun shines,
when your body melts
into mine I'll feel my heart expand
& the parentheses around things
fall off into piles of little black crescents
like rinds of moons gone bad.

5.

What fun awaits us
as we go for a Sunday drive
across the border, the yellow fields
of the river deltas full of cows
& fundamentalists. *God!* wants everything
to be the way it is. *God!* wants you
to send your money now.
Small brown birds line the tree branches
like a Christmas carol, traffic flows
past the red exemplary barns
of Fantasy Gardens. God's a text residing
between the lines & some are nervous
playing Name the Invisible. We exist as one
between pregnancies, otherwise inhabited
by a spirit whose limbs we watch
on the video screen as a play of darknesses
in the water. This is the head, this is a leg,
this pulsing smudge is the heart.
Or a string of smudges in the case of
a litter, Mother Cat with transmitters
on her belly. Sea rose, sea iris, sea lily:
three sisters of a mystical landscape
revealed by H.D. who named her child Perdita,
imagine. Listen to the story
of the girls who were dragged
kicking & screaming out of the convents
to go back home after the Reformation.
The lucky ones eventually returned
to live out their days *virgo intacta.*
Nobody new was allowed to enter.

6.

To change the subject
the ornamental façade
is back with a vengeance, even though
our pictorial muscles are not
what they used to be.
Houses, one to a lot. Green
surrounds, car out front.
The changing light does not change
the facts. Says the cheerful shopper
to the food-store cashier, The wife
sent me out for this, she's making
one of those salads with green jelly
all in a circle (celery, two apples,
carrots, a package of chopped walnuts).
New Year's Eve.
The alleys patrolled by Italian labourers,
their dumptrucks filled with pebbles
that make a prodigious sound as they issue
into the wheelbarrows of Angelini's
Drainage. A new house going up,
piles of dead-looking dirt surround.
Someone's wash on the line straddles
a frozen garden, grotesque spikes
of brussels sprouts, mad-hatter growths
of cabbage and broccoli, blackened
under a cold breath's beard of frost.
The stones clatter, wet ground gapes.

8.

Night's dreams
persist into day, writer as satyr
in the front seat of a taxi aroused
& full of intent, remembered
dreams not black & white but the colour
of a rainy night, dreams *noir*, with smoke
that coils under the hat brims
of lonely detectives. "Don't know much
about *his*-tory, don't know much
bi-*ol*-ogy." Going in & out of rooms,
making the bed, putting on the *Goldberg*
Variations, then the CBC
The turquoise globe tilts towards the east.
My imaginary red beret matches my imaginary
red stockings, a walking signal
to the Resistance.
The underground is brightly lit,
is *Hades* of an entrepreneurial spirit
full of misery imports from horrible countries,
thin shiny garments hanging on mannequins
whose bony hips are slung
with silver belts, meagre Madonnas
remote and on tiptoe,
their white oval faces
stamped with hope, passivity, and sorrow.

9.

Myriad drops cling to myriad twigs
on the neighbour's birch tree, the neighbour
actually three, each a blond, none of them
home very much. Their tree
like a large weed wending
its lanky crooked way upward
in the forest a mere stick
you'd never notice. Still, it touches
the way trees in the city do, a place
in us that lives in books & dreams
that we forget & have to be reminded
to hug our kid. Everything
impossible to put off even on Sunday
which seems to be a colder day
than any other and gives you time
for the personals: what we do
and say, and what settles between
like, don't bother with those dishes,
I'll do them later. Or the sound
of your voice talking long-distance
to your mother I hear
coming inside from out rain-soaked and
always hungry this time of day.
How was it? you say.
The daily is an engine of these
and other particulars, exactnesses
like the way you sit on the sofa
with that book that pen
and will never again
in that way, that light, just so
many grey hairs in your hair as today,
how many peels it took
to peel your morning orange.

10.

How different they are from us
I say speaking of the French in movies,
how I envy their expressions
& their clothes, their kisses
the size of documentaries.
The way they talk on the phone
you can tell they are undiminished
by technology. The Divine Fools
who live on our corner
& drive rainbow-coloured vehicles
will soon see me pass
with a black umbrella
over my head & a letter in my hand,
stamp shining in the upper right corner,
as the day dims and vapours accumulate
on McKenzie Heights.
The last of the Christmas trees
have been undressed and discarded
like victims in the alleys.
I spoke to ours, I said Thanks,
you smelled great, your beauty
made us happy. Imagine bringing a tree
into the house to adorn with coloured lights
and tiny birds and bending angels –
to offer our anxious gifts to, sacrifices
of love and obligation.

Common Sense

The wind is a lack
manifesting
hair all over the place.
A hunched posture. Trees bending
like women by a river.

Oh the swell
tide of desire
comes & goes, I run
upstairs –
wanting to write but –
listen to imaginary lawnmowers
instead, the glimmer
of voices from the radio –

Remembering early spring up north,
elastic mud, soft ice
blossoming to webs
under our shoes
precise imprints – like dreams
recorded in tiny writing.

Image or prophecy,
which way to read them?
That one is the other
finds a blind spot in me –

The sun is setting. So what,
it's its job.

Rosary

In small rivers
of hours
passing

words grab
as fingers
spread the air

when leaning
down to stretch
interior ligaments

that pull at, hurt
a little
behind the mind –

It feels good
to do this & breathe
coming up

counting pebble
by pebble
my spine

Summer

The house is built
day by day
quickly, the trucks

come & go
with shirtless operators
cranes & gears

the roof on
(prefab)
in one morning

now the pale yellow
siding, imitation brick
along the front

it is obviously
grand, he is
proud, entering

the unfinished
front door, a small
uncomplaining man

to look over
his day's work,
try the lights

V

THE PANGS OF SUNDAY: NEW POEMS

The Parrot

She flew, she was up
& gone, they had let her out
for a treat & were sorry now.
Red tail feathers
way, way up in a fir tree
on the side of a mountain.
It was north. Crows
eyed her. Way, way down
the people were making
little pyramids of peanuts &
calling her name: Isabel! Isabel!
They clicked their tongues
and whistled, they went away and
came back later. The sun got large
and red, turned the heat up
under her vocabulary. Later
they could hear her exhortations
to the moonlight: Hey Sailor!
Good Golly Miss Molly! Want
A Cracker? So What!
The crows backed off
& stared, diamond bracelets dangling
from their beaks. All that night
the parrot prayed & sang,
in the morning it was over.
She glided downward, branch
to spiky branch. The people
wept and applauded, rushed her
back to her cage exhausted,
the undisputed champion
of the air. She was never the same
after that. The vet said it was
a bit like the cave scene
in *A Passage to India* – something

to do with language, the dark &
existence. Stupendous!
the parrot kept saying for years
after & the crows invented a red dream.

Winter and Then Summer

Wet grey roof of heaven, turning world
to judge's chambers, to nervous agreements
with the sun who will appear wanly and brief
counting out bronchitis pills.
                                        This morning
the music faltered in the tape deck
until halfway over the bridge then
came on strong as a whiff
of Napoleon brandy, made me want to
be somewhere else, forgetting
my office and the boring desolate
classrooms smelling of apple cores & rain.

Someday soon it will be June
& we'll all be happy, our happiness tinkling
like windchimes on a summer porch at night,
the full moon backing up to a star
like a truck to a dairy, to receive
the milk of human kindness. You and me
we'll turn the pages of our novels,
wave away the bees, kiss each other
for the millionth time.

Even now the chimes make live music
with the wind and the rain. On my tongue
a faint aftertaste of white rum & green salsa,
a dream of a silky dress on a hot piano night
with wet stars leaning out of the sky,
low in front, soft and tight.

Peter's Room

Conversations
are short,
stalling on tape spools
& thin brown tongues
of cassettes, in there
the glad weight of music
& dull inquiries always
backing out, Listen
to this, you say
bending toward controls
& I do. From across
the street they can see
us listening, talk
reduced to essentials:
Let's go downtown tomorrow.
Buy blue sheets, onion bagels.

The Move

Across the street the moving van
waits agape for things. Our burdens
made actual: this lamp
held by the base, pathetic
in the daylight, trailing
its twisted cord. A peculiar
stain abashed in the sun,
the blank smeared face of the TV
set, the shocked houseplants &
grinning bedclothes yet hold their virtue
in our anxious expressions, our old
clothes on, a reconsidered hat.

Poem for Norbert's Thesis

Norbert tests the wind recovering
whatever place is for him to see
and say as place, in terms we argue we need
to round the edges of, pat form
into the middle, that form being female
and of stature such as a Queen
enthroned in milky skies of Egypt –
his place to hear songs, words
as bushes and squirrels and small mosses
under the sun in breezes of their own are a choir
of angels. He may dispute "angels" but not
their reality, the long ovals of their dark
open mouths over songbooks the size
of surveyors' maps, their white nighties
and bare feet. Landscape, that troubled
word when it leads to beauty, which
is also a sea, whose metaphors lift
and fall like chromatic scales
in the difficulty of our bodies.

Emergency

Words, constraints
evaporate in my mouth
or they wound me
with many small wounds –
a rash of pygmy arrows
tainted with a numbing sleep

In which I dream a dragon
lifts me into all his amphibian arms,
ceases his vaporous bellowing
& gazes into my throat.

Birds, insects falter.
Animals slide into damp grass, weed-tips
quiver from the roots on up.

Talk to me, I thought
& didn't say as the wounding of words
swallows its own tongue
& nearly dies. Human love
is not so easy as speech
will allow. All
the forms of it embrace awkwardly
beside the ambulance
& nobody knows what to do.

Portrait

My father & brother
upstream fishing. Brook trout.
1957? A bottle of pop
hot from the trunk of the car,
mother bending over
something – baby sister?
Or the sun hats, the Noxzema.
I cast a line toward the creek
left-handed in the twinkling shade.
Something like the Dryads murmur.
No-see-ums murmur.
The brook babbling too
but no radio. Father's voice
announcing four trout
or five. Up on the road
a Sunday Studebaker
explodes dust toward
a beige & purple mountain,
and someone asks where
the hot dog buns are and a square
tablecloth is laid on the grass
which is sharp & filled
with buzzing.

Ghost Dance

The chemistry instructor
rounds the corner
holding his plastic molecule
up in the rain, all red
gears & balls like tinker toys,
collapsible. It glows
like truth in the drear
month of The Dead, each atom
dancing a ghost dance
of its own, nucleus vibrating.
The rain falls,
the Free Enterprise zones
of British Columbia
give themselves a round of applause
as the chemistry instructor
totes his molecule
& his trench coat to the classroom,
spinning out formulas
in white chalk, knotted yarns
in the sleeve of God's hidden laughter.

Doubletalk

One-eyed one-tongued night
yield me a trace of myself,
that I was in Montreal
briefly, before Derrida
and *différance* crashed into English –
give me back the metro
the winter park
the red shoes I wore
swinging my purse, my heart
in the wrong place –
before it got so complicated to
speak you'd just as soon
leave it all in the original,
mute and appealing. First
you have woman and then you have poet,
then Catholic or Protestant,
Mary or no Mary, then your bi-*langue*
country not to mention the
country of your soft & lingual body –
yield me a trace of myself
when I took the bus down Sherbrooke
with my little bit of French
and my red shoes & longed for his sweet
poison kisses and missed him
with my unanimous tongue,
my singularly untrue heart
thinking *je t'aime, je t'aime.*

Mythology

With car windows open
on a summer night
the air smells like fish
& an art deco moon
does a balancing act
on the top hat of City Hall –

At the break of night's
yellowing horizon this moon
silverplates someone's destiny, let's say
yours and mine

As if going west
toward those dark blue mountains
made an Egyptian boat
of your worn-out Renault
and we its captive souls
borne along borne along
through the lowing sky

Craning our stiff necks
as we pass the other boatloads
who crane their necks in return,
our shouts

Catapult across the galaxies
& our flashlights are little pinpoints
in the great dark that receives
with open mouth the endless tale
of our lives.

The Scalpel

Repeatedly the doctors told him
the artery was badly clogged –
the blue one in the side
of everyone's neck that counts
the beats in a warm hollow,
where the scalpel travels
a long samurai motion
in the gloved hand
of the Japanese surgeon, "a man
of few words" according to my father
who woke up, glad to see
the ceiling. "You think you're
going to die," he said & then
the ceiling & cold stainless light.

Outside, a young forsythia
puts out pale green shoots
& the snow lies beyond, in patches –
a motley scarface world out there
& a fresh sad cut in the skin
of paradise.

Last night, he said,
the old man beside him was trying
to leave. "Get me out of here!"
he called out, repetitious
& unmindful of the hour –
"Get me out of here!"

And today the old man is sleeping
& my father, glum in slippers and robe
ticks off tomorrow's menu sheet

looking out beyond the TV set
at tender green forsythia
getting a grip
on slippery weather.

Guys

Hazed in as the weather changes
into something a little looser & brings
us a drink, dims the lights.
Trees show their undersides as the wind
ruffles them all over. It's supper time
but we aren't hungry, having eaten
two pounds of firm sweet cherries
& half a loaf of French bread between
4:30 and 5:00. Afterward I nearly dozed off
sitting in the sun on the porch with the dog
like someone's teenage sister in 1961. Immense
shiny cars cruise by with guys hanging out the window.
Did I want to go for a ride, they inquired.
I was just sitting on the porch after eating too many
cherries at once. My lips and teeth are black,
index fingers dyed purple, we
devoured them straight out of the sink,
I'm amazed we even bothered washing them, at least
we never used to – when kids with apples we just
wiped the DDT off on the hip of our shorts
and bit in. At supper, baby carrots
and green beans and on the porch
zinc washtubs full of ears of corn trailing
blonde tresses like dismembered princess brides
I married off to princely invisible grooms.
And they were happy as the day is long
and went on plane trips & saw out the window
the jigsaw fields of prairie drought &
journalists in expense account 4 × 4's
gathering footage for the six o'clock news.

Skip to My Lou

Some exchanges today, mostly money
for goods, raspberries a nice old man
sold me not quite ripe yet, dark pink, mounded
in a used yogurt container, clean raspberries,
dry papery hands my change counted into
quarter by quarter until it reached two dollars.
Clouds in the sky resembling slow horses.
Ideas for bouquets suggest themselves
like happy whores in a Western movie walking by
corner store flowers on my way to the doctor's.
Their big bare feet and brassy eyes,
serving up the anaesthetic on a tray, white
skirts, bottles flying in a fistfight, crashing,
crashing. Doctor lets me off the table
& I lift my bangs in the mirror
to see the Band-Aid where she took
the biopsy and gave me back a piece of my skin
in a small jar writing "pathology" on it, would I
mind, the lab is on my way to buy you a tie & I'm
not to worry about anything. In the mirror,
considering, I hold a striped tie up to myself &
down it goes so far I feel like the fat man on a chair
with legs wide apart, a small hat on, answering questions
with jokes. The mirror itself revives an aroma,
cobalt-blue cologne bottles, powder puffs stained
the colour of flesh, an oval box of hairpins, pungent
traces of dandruff on silvery tweezers. The way skin
fills our rooms, our tombs, the way it is alive.
I'm glad they took my cheque. I'm glad you liked the tie.

My Favourite Science

Fork lightning, arterial tributaries,
a bare tree in the park in November
when the sky is ochre, making a Rome
of McKenzie Heights, and the Sublime
of a Nissan wax job parked on the street,
and an absence of kites or any such foolishness
in the air, claiming for appearances some
sombre function: the way energy branches out,
the way lights go on elongated through the rain
drops on the window, stylized stars of Bethlehem
hovering like white nuns over an unwed mother's
bundle of joy.

Elegy, the Fertility Specialist

He gave it to me straight
and I had to thank him
for the information, the percentages
that dwindled in his pencil writing
hand. I watched them drop
from 70, to 40, to 20
as all the variables were added in
and even after 20 he made a question mark. I felt
doors closing in swift silent succession
as I passed each checkpoint on the way
to the cold awful ruler, expert astronomer,
charterer of heavenly colonies,
answerer of questions, and this question
Could we have a child? and this answer, No
I don't think so. Oh
of course he could go in there
and have a look if I really wanted,
steer his ship around the fraying edges
of my terrain, peering with his spyglass,
cross-hatching impediments on his diagram
of the uterine pear & its two branching filaments:
he wouldn't recommend it, he would say,
squeezing his spyglass shut and putting it back
in its maroon velvet box. We make the usual
small gestures of disappointment
as if we'd run out of luck in a ticket line
and I say goodbye
and walk past the receptionist
busy at her files and it is
as if something with wings was crushing itself
to my heart, to comfort
or to be comforted I didn't know which
or even what it was, some angel, and
entered the elevator with the gabbing nurses

going down to lunch and a little girl
in a sun-dress, her delicate
golden shoulders stencilled from the straps
of her bathing suit: a perfect white X.

Boat of the Dead

Matisse's white doves perch atop the birdcage
and one in the hand permits
a close examination of its resemblance
to the Holy Spirit. *One woman's obsession*
the reviewer wrote about every book he reviewed.
In them was blood and repetition
for no one can help it writing
that way, a woman. She lifts her dripping head
from the sink – excuse me, her dripping *hair* –
and wraps it in a pink monogrammed towel. In the
fairness of today's weather noon approaches
and proffers pastrami on rye with a pickle beside.
Scent of blackberries, ascending the path, scent
of blackberries and squashed blond grass spread apart
over earth's pubis. Right here
the four elements come together
with their relatives the horses
whose long necks are exactly
the right length for eating
the grass. And when they look up,
a white ferry is passing over earth's divine
curvature of the spine, the traffic of self-infatuated
commerce, goal-oriented, dependent on radar,
but missing the skin of something,
missing touch.

September, Turning, the Long Road Down to Love

The turning leaves
turn in a wind that rises
as if something warm,
invisible, and female just got up
from a nap and, half-dreaming,
walked to the kitchen
to make a cup of tea: Orange Pekoe?
Ruby Mist? Earl Grey? which one
did she choose? How about
Ruby Mist agree the women zipping up
their handbags at the airport
and boarding a propellered plane
from whose window porthole heights
topography is listless & small
lucite lakes gather in the deep corners
of mountains, as if assembled
for a meeting. The lakes speak
to one another over the white heads
of the mountains and this for them is like
dealing with the patriarchy. Ah,
the patriarchy, we sigh, having reached
our destination. We button up
our sweaters as the wind rises
and twirls the drying leaves
like you'd turn a wineglass
to look into the red depths and make
a fine judgement. The long
taproots of these rustling
turning trees that stand as a company of
completed metamorphoses of the human body
(branches for arms, bark for skin)
tap a little more love

for language to replace us with, who talk
among the mountains, and talk
with only ourselves, and history,
and the example of the evening
to blame for our silences.

Bear Bracelet

Silver bracelet smears the ink, blue-black, of my new pen
toward a postcard of California. The squeeze being on, veins
pulsate blue-black in the map of my back, wrists, temples
thinking. The bracelet bangs along the table and keeps me
company. If I joined a Sweat Lodge to sit and sweat with others
poetry would come to me on the wings of a great bird but as it is,
bear visage, Haida, ambles along pigeon-toed
out of the bush. Blue-black veins crossing mounds of knuckles,
mountain passes under the moon of wintertime, mounds
of sleeping bears. Pressing on, in a direction,
sort of, toward the great curve of beach, blue & westward
of clear days & better weather – the waking bears
stunned and thin preparing for the light.

Demonstration Model

Kiss in the leaf-dappled room
among dinner plates littered
with the purplish thigh bones of chickens, club
soda going flat in blue glasses,
a Lockjaw Davis tape over the swish
of traffic & phlegm-flight of motorcycle,
heels clenched to black metal. Feel the fall
of heat upon the earth, upon the redhead sunbathing
across the street like a dame in a detective
novel behind important shrubbery, the scent
of lilacs you're going to steal after it gets
dark, just a few. Frail empty heads
of dandelions line the real estate
where dogs play nipping at each other's jugular
& the demonstration models test their curves
and brakes, lurching up side streets,
the clutch confused & upset, soon
to have a price written in soap on the windshield
under gold & fuchsia banners where the wind blows.

Chicken in a Pensive Shell

Is really Chicken in a Pineapple Shell, but
glancing at it sideways
while making tea I thought it said,
in a Pensive Shell, a mood
I'm often in, coming from thoughts, my
face dark with them as a pansy's.

Pascal in his *Pensées*
says nothing about chicken
but is sure our major distress
derives from having a home, the same old
boring old place where we rot &
rot and thereby hangs a tale.
Of woe, according to Pascal's
pensée, and here it's almost time
to start the chicken, Poulet
Marengo, a favourite
of Napoleon's. He liked it garnished
with crawfish and fried eggs.

As the oven heats up, rosy elements
brighten the tinted window
you look in to see your
nervous soufflé rising or not. No
pensée will help your soufflé
or chicken either, bubbling like lava
in the orange pot, with eight mushrooms,
a cup of white wine, and the empty pineapple
shells arrayed for next time, or next year,
or never. Their pensive moods
attract the wrong sort of chicken
who wear black thongs and carry a knife.
Their shirts are shiny, they belong
to another page, another life.

I prefer my Poulet ungarnished,
with rice, an easy salad on the side.
In a pensive shell will lie
my thoughts, dark inside
where you can't see the ocean
that roars and roars
in Napoleon's sleep. He spread himself
too thin. His crawfish garnish
outmanoeuvred him. I rest my case
on the kitchen counter where books
outnumber saucers & adjacent recipes
clash by night in pineapple shell
rowboats. And Divan gets a whiff
of Marengo and bam! the Duke
of Wellington fires his cannon.

For Carson McCullers at 30

Crept the day sideways through the shutters
and disposed of night. Morning coffee outdoors
reading and having a smoke when a man arrives
to take your picture. Your teeth
feel suddenly awful, arms awkward
in a white blouse on the table's edge,
mind busy with the stranger who lays his
suitcase on the doorstep & with a flourish
produces a hairbrush, a shammy for your shoes.
Your eyes lock over their waxed & dented leather,
the sky a smooth unpuckered grey, hot as blazes.

In the garden the photographer lays his
cigarette down beside some black equipment
and squinches his eye to the viewfinder,
his hat off, the gallant white parting
in his hair lifting at a 40-degree angle.
You give him the side of your face
as if it were your last dime and he
was about to spend it on a chocolate bar
for your beautiful, sullen cousin.

Animals

When I come out of the bathroom
animals are waiting in the hall
and when I settle down to read
an animal comes between me
and my book and when I put on
a fancy dinner, a few animals
are under the table staring at the guests,
and when I mail a letter
or go to the Safeway there's always
an animal tagging along
or crying left at home and when I get
home from work animals leap joyously
around my old red car so I feel like
an avatar with flowers & presents all over
her body, and when I dance around
the kitchen at night wild & feeling
lovely as Margie Gillis, the animals
try to dance too, they stagger on
back legs and open their mouths, pink
and black and fanged, and I take their paws
in my hands and bend toward them,
happy and full of love.

My Horse and I

I rode my lovely horse
into the perfume department
at Eaton's. This looked
exactly the way you would imagine.
My horse was a little afraid
& I had to kick his sides gently
from time to time with my heels
as we passed the oceans of Eternity
and Opium, Infinitude and Beautiful.
It was lightning purple weather
& my horse was lonely for Wyoming.
We tried not to break anything
but also we were not abstract,
we were not a video. As I said,
I rode my lovely horse
into the perfume department
at Eaton's.